Water, Water, Everywhere

by **MARY BETH SPANN**

With the Editors of

SO-AGV-924

Table of Contents

Chapter 1

Water: Three Ways

Here's a riddle:

> What can be hard and sparkly as glass, or soft and wet as a summer shower, or almost invisible?

If you guessed "water," then you are right.

Ice is hard. Rainwater is wet. Steam is almost invisible. Like all **matter**, water has three **states,** or forms. These states of water are **solid, liquid,** and **gas.**

Ice is water in its solid state. Rainwater is water in its liquid state. Steam is water in the form of a gas called **water vapor.**

Water changes from one form to another because of temperature. When it is very cold, liquid water freezes and becomes a solid—ice. When liquid water gets very, very hot, it boils and turns into steam—a gas. When the air around ice gets warmer, the ice melts and changes back into a liquid. Cool air makes the steam change back into a liquid. All the time it is the same water. Yet the water is in three different states.

Chapter 2

Shape and Volume

A good way to compare the three states of water is to look at their shape and their **volume**. Volume is how much space matter takes up.

Water as a liquid

Water as a solid

Water as a gas

Solids Stay the Same

Solids hold their shape and their volume. When you put an ice cube in a bowl, it just sits there. It looks like a cube. If you put the same ice cube in a cup, it still looks the same and still takes up the same amount of space. Its shape and volume do not change.

Liquids Change Shape, Not Volume

A liquid can change shape. But it cannot change volume. When you pour water into a bowl, it takes the shape of the bowl. When you pour the same water into a cup, it takes the shape of the cup. As long as the cup is big enough, the water will stay put. But if you have more water than the cup can hold, it will spill over the top. There is nothing you can do to make it fit into a space that is too small. That is because you cannot change the volume of a liquid.

Gases Change Shape and Volume

Gases change shape, too. But they can also change volume. A large amount of gas can be squeezed to fit into a small container. If you put the same amount of gas in a bigger container, it will spread out to the edges of the container. In fact, if you take the lid off a pan of boiling water, the steam—water in the form of gas—will leave the pan and spread out into the air.

Chapter 3

How the Molecules Behave

At first glance, each state of water—solid, liquid, and gas—looks and feels very different from the other two states. Rain looks different from steam. Steam would never be mistaken for an icicle. A pile of snow looks nothing like a lake full of water.

Yet, looking at rainwater, steam, and ice under a microscope tells a different story. The smallest particles of water—called **molecules**—look alike, no matter what state the water is in.

Icicles are frozen water. This is water in its solid state.

If water molecules are all alike, why do liquid water, solid water, and water as a gas look and behave so differently? It has to do with how molecules move. In fact, molecules are always moving, even in something like a solid block of ice.

Solids Are Slow

If water molecules held a race, the solid water molecules would come in last. Solid water molecules move more slowly than gas or liquid water molecules. They also tend to stay crowded together as they move.

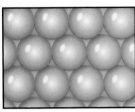

Water molecules in their solid state are slow-moving and crowded together.

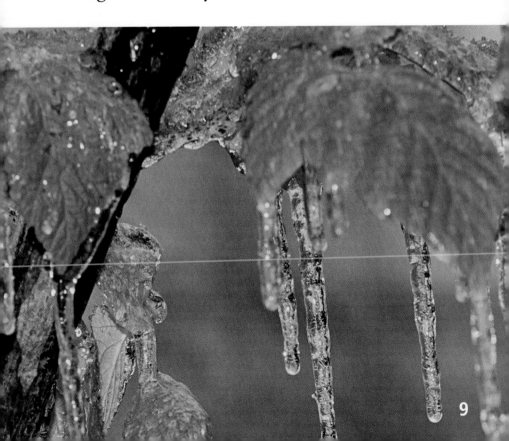

Liquids Are Quicker

In the same race, liquid water molecules would come in second. They move more quickly than those in solid water. They also spread farther apart from each other than solid water molecules.

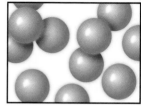

Water molecules in their liquid state move freely and are not so crowded.

Rain is water in its liquid state.

The steam from a train is water in the form of a gas.

Gas Is Fast!

Gas molecules would win the water molecule race. They are the fastest of all! They move around quickly compared to the molecules in solid or liquid water. When these gas molecules travel, they really spread out. There is no crowding together for them!

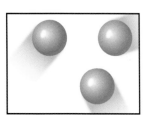

Water molecules as a gas are fast-moving and spread far apart.

Chapter 4

The Water-Go-Round

There is only a limited supply of water on Earth.
Much of the water that was here long ago is the
same water that is here today. The water we have is
constantly changing, moving, and being used over
again. This process is called the **water cycle.**

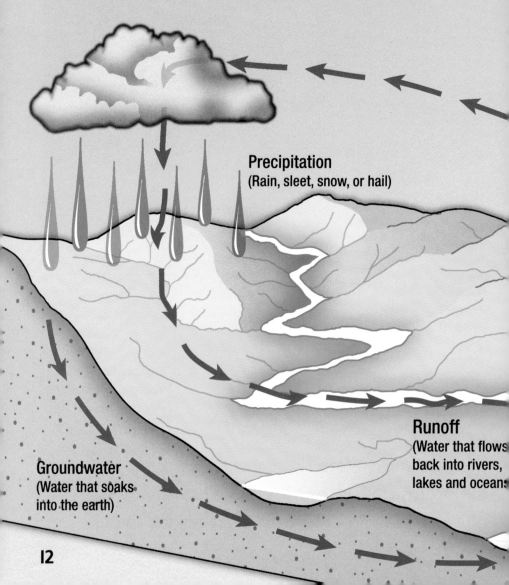

Precipitation
(Rain, sleet, snow, or hail)

Runoff
(Water that flows
back into rivers,
lakes and oceans

Groundwater
(Water that soaks
into the earth)

Heat is the fuel that makes the water cycle begin. The Sun's heat warms the liquid water in Earth's oceans, lakes, and rivers—and anywhere else there is water. When the liquid water gets warm enough, it turns into water vapor. The water vapor rises into the air and forms clouds. When a cloud gets cool enough, the water vapor begins to turn back into liquid. The liquid water molecules clump together. They get heavier and heavier until the cloud cannot hold them any longer. The water falls back to Earth in the form of rain, sleet, hail, or snow. The water travels back to the oceans, lakes, and rivers, and the water cycle begins again.

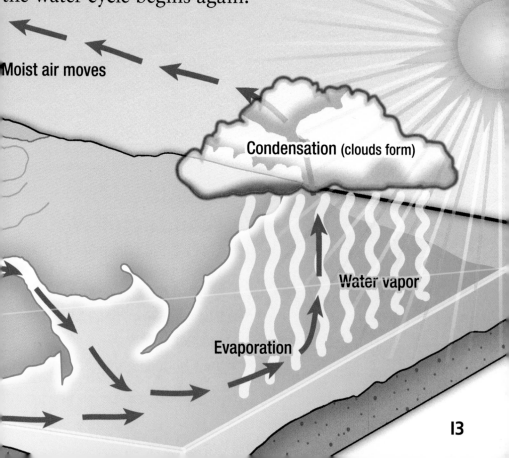

Moist air moves

Condensation (clouds form)

Water vapor

Evaporation

The water cycle never stops. Whether as a solid, liquid, or gas, Earth's water is constantly being reused. That is a very good thing. People, animals, and plants all need water to live and grow.

Wonderful Water
- Earth is the only planet in which all three states of water exist at the same time.
- Water covers 70% of Earth's surface.
- Your body is about 70% water.

Glossary

gas (GAS) matter that has no definite shape or volume *(page 2)*

liquid (LIK-wid) matter that has a definite volume but not a definite shape *(page 2)*

matter (MAT-uhr) anything that takes up space and has mass *(page 2)*

molecule (MOL-uh-kyewl) smallest part matter can be broken into *(page 8)*

solid (SOL-id) matter that has a definite shape and volume *(page 2)*

state (STAYT) a form of matter *(page 2)*

volume (VOL-yewm) how much space matter takes up *(page 4)*

water cycle (WAW-tuhr SIGH-kuhl) movement of Earth's water over and over from a liquid to a gas and back *(page 12)*

water vapor (WAW-tuhr VAY-puhr) water as a gas in the atmosphere *(page 3)*

Index